CH00500724

Platform 7
by Sammy Nour

Cover designed by Grace Jenkinson
Cover photography by Andrew Lee

Proudly published July 2021 in Leicester, UK,
by SanRoo Publishing,
26 Bramble Way, Leicester, LE3 2GY, U.K.
www.sanroopublishing.co.uk

ISBN 978-0-9957078-5-6

Contents

Foreword

I'd like to thank you, thank you for buying this book and supporting the arts. If you bought it after seeing me perform then double thank you! Art is such an important aspect of mine and many others' lives so the support we give each other is vital for creative outlets to flourish.

I hope you enjoy this book of my poetry. It will take you on the journey of my development as a spoken word artist and performer. From my first ever spoken word piece, Twenty Six Pounds Seventy P, to the most recently written poem in this book, Cracks, and everything in between.

My literary journey started in secondary school, when I, like many, wrote because the teachers made us write for some piece of work or another. One day we had to write a story about an alien invasion, as we had been reading *Chocky* by John Wyndham. I wrote the introduction to my story, not thinking much of it. In the following lesson the English teacher, Mrs Cuthbertson, read what I had written with such passion and vigour that I was literally speechless. She gave me such praise that I started to believe I could write. That story ended up being several pages of A4 and she loved every word. From then on, I had the passion, desire, and belief to write, and found I was really interested in it. I will always be grateful to that wonderful teacher, Mrs Cuthbertson, for helping me discover my love of writing.

As a teenager I wrote many songs for the band I used to play in. It never occurred to me until later on that this was just poetry put to music. Long after I stopped playing in a band I would write poetry, always thinking in my mind that they were song lyrics. Then one day in 2008 I was getting the train back to university in Liverpool from Leicester, and got stuck on the bike compartment of a train for most of my journey. I was so angry. The whole way there I was just having this rant in my head that was rhyming and when I got home, I wrote it all down. I thought of it more of a rap really than anything else.

A few years later, I went to Shambala festival and decided to go into the spoken word tent. We sat and listened to several poets and rappers and I really enjoyed most of what I heard. About half way through the performances I thought, 'hang on a minute, I have loads of material like this. Maybe I can have a go'. When I got home, I dug out that rant from the train that day and started practicing and reciting it. I mentioned wanting to perform at work and one of the TAs there was really into spoken word. She recommended that I visit some open mic events. At random I picked Jawdance at Richmix. I learnt my poem off by heart and signed up to perform.

When I got there, I was instantly terrified. Richmix is a big venue with a huge stage and really bright lights shining on the performers. There were also a lot of people there. Only then did I realise that you didn't have to have memorised your piece, but I was determined to perform it without reading the copy I had in my back pocket just in case. The piece I performed was my rant from the train that day, Twenty Five Pounds Seventy P, now fashioned into a spoken word piece. It got a good applause and as I left the stage the host shook my hand and said,

"That was wicked!" From that moment on I wanted to write and perform more.

I still cringe a little bit at that poem, in particular the obvious rhyming and relentlessness of it. Looking back at that piece and comparing it to what I write now, I feel I have developed as both a writer and performer, but still think I have a long way to go.

As I wrote and performed more, I began to develop a style and even started getting booked for gigs, either supporting or as the featured artist. It felt great to have that creative outlet and be able to showcase what I had written. That was it, I have loved spoken word since then.

Special thanks goes out to everyone who has influenced and nurtured my writing over the years. From those who have critiqued my performances, my writing, and given me constructive feedback, to those who have put events on to give people a chance to develop and practise their skills, to all my friends, girlfriends and family who have just listened to my poetry or come to see me perform. Without all these people my performances and writing would not be the same.

I would like to give a special mention to those who have put on events. You have been such a big part of my life and helped me to form my own spoken word night, Some-Antics. In particular, thanks to Jenny 'Hibword' Hibberd of House of Verse, Andrew Lee of Heard of Mouth, Richard 'Bass Ventura' Lloyd of Beat It Open Jam, Lydia Towsey of Word, and Kishan 'Zeropence' Anand of Anerki, co- founder and organiser of Some-Antics.

All these events and your encouragement have

helped to advance not only my development, but that of many others in the Midlands' poetry and music scenes. I can't thank you enough. I like to think I picked up the baton from you, in putting on a welcoming event with an ethos and vibe that will allow people to grow and develop, as well as having loads of fun at the same time.

A massive thank you to Sandra Pollock and Jerusha Barnett-Cameron of SanRoo Publishing for all your support and belief, Andrew Lee for your creativity and insight in shooting the pictures, Mark Grist for taking the time to read my drafts and give me feedback, and Grace Jenkinson for your great work on the cover designs. *Platform 7* would be nothing without you.

So, *Platform 7* is the journey so far. From that first performance in 2012 to Cracks in 2019. It's worth bearing in mind that these poems are written to be spoken. So in print they can read a little awkwardly at times, but I hope you enjoy them all the same.

I present to you: *Platform 7*.

STILL STANDING

The rocks, the hill, the climb.
One more floor up on
the staircase in my mind.
One stage closer
in the search for what
I'm trying to find.

An old church.
A castle lies in its ruins.
But atop of the hill
it still stands.

It still stands.

It still stands
just like I still stand.
But I can't say the same
for my best laid plans.

'I'm the Prince of Valencia!'
At the summit a child cries.
Mesmerised I was
by the conviction
in his eyes.

'Keep that dream alive, young man,
you'll get there one day.'
I said,
'keep that dream alive, young man.
Don't let the king
get in your way.'

INNOCENCE

I don't normally hate on
people who are innocent.
But I'm a football fan,
and you can probably
guess where this is going…

But what is innocent?
Is cruising around town looking for girls
too drunk to stand in chip shops
the behaviour of someone with
innocent intentions?

"An idiot on a night out
but a top bloke,"
some Blades decry.

Are you innocent, Mr Footballer?
I don't know,
I wasn't there.
But I do care
about a woman's right to be.
About a female's right
to go to the chippy
and not be the subject
of a phone call between
two blokes saying
"I've got a girl."

I've voiced my objections
I've called for his rejection.
Other fans call me a traitor.
My personal favourite is
"When he scores facing the kop

will you not celebrate?"
But I tell you now
if the man scores the winning goal
in an FA Cup final,
it will always be tainted.

Whether he did or didn't rape her,
is not my point.
Are our morals so disjointed that
we support this man's behaviour?
Do we want our sons to grow up
thinking drunk women
are there to be taken?
Hunted like prey?
Led to a car
and whisked away?

Why can't a drunk female get
a greasy chip butty
without being subjected
to your guilty intentions?

Admittedly for me
overturning the guilty verdict
was unexpected.
But if you're as innocent
as you claim you are,
why did you leave the hotel
by the fire exit?
Why did, when you entered
the hotel, you tell a lie?
This doesn't sound like the behaviour
of a man who has nothing to hide.

And it's not uncommon,
I won't deny it.
Back to your place with a girl,

she passes out 'cos she's pissed.
Do you still try it?

Hell no if you respect the opposite sex,
hell no if you have morals to vex.
This is fucking basic.
Having to even state this in 2018
makes me frustrated.
In these days of me two, me three,
me four, five and more,
three and a half billion tales
of behaviour to deplore.
What I'm saying fellow Blades
is see past the fact he
was found innocent in court.
Don't we want the next generation
to grow up with more positive thought?
If that's the case we must set an example,
stick to our values with no disclaimer preamble.

I know it's sad we live in times where our
heroes and statues are being
torn down across lands.
You're disappointed to learn
he's another fallen hero,
with guilt on his hands.

But be brave and be bold,
let's not get it confused,
don't stick up for the abusers,
stick up for the abused.
We can make this world
a better place for our women,
we can make the world
a better place for our people,
on the terrace of the football ground
where the story begins.

Have your own mind,
don't be led by the pack.
Stand your ground,
even when your opinion's attacked.
Treat women with the
respect they deserve.
Imagine that was a loved one,
before you defend the absurd.

So yes, Mr Footballer, I respect
that you may be innocent
in the eyes of our justice system.

But in the eyes of
innocence
and real men,
you are
unforgiven.

A COUNCIL HOUSE IN EARLSFIELD

I remember, a council house in Earlsfield,
not far from Tooting Broadway,
was where my Irish Nan lived.
I look through memory's glade.

She would meet us at the doorway,
a smile danced across her face.
No words could ever simulate
her whole-hearted embrace.

It was a small affair,
a green adorned the square.
Dolly Parsons lived next door,
I had not a worry or a care.

Sometimes I'd look through the window,
as my Nan would make me toast.
I looked forward to apple pie,
enjoyed after Sunday roast.

She would always have a smile,
very rarely have a moan.
She was cheery all the while,
I suspect even when left alone.

Through a life well-worn,
she had certainly soldiered through.
She had a certain disposition
that made us happy too.

Sometimes she'd sip a Baileys
and tell us stories old.

We'd listen so attentively,
as history would unfold.

That old red phone next to the stairs,
never made me feel far from home.
It was the only home from home,
where I was never too scared to sleep alone.

That council house in Earlsfield,
so many memories linked.
The aging, faded wallpaper,
my nana's cheeky wink.

LAND OF MY FATHER

The land of my father is a beautiful place
but if it were a person there'd be tears on its face,
with the wrong fitting shoes and one odd lace.

A human with a history of depression,
with too many scars to give each one a mention.
It would be someone with a tendency for violence,
one of those people who always suffers in silence.

Someone who has a warped state of mind,
with a tendency for soul-searching all the time.
The kind who always argues with the other,
even though the other is their own brother.

Case notes read: big trust issues,
emotional, always carries a box of tissues.
One of those people no-one can be bothered with,
because their fight is too brutal,
carried out with fists and not oven-mitts.

Friendly by nature, but became a hater
brought up in the wrong part of town.
Changed by watching their children drown -
die needlessly as the hospital cabinet ran dry.

A person who has shoulder pain
from having their arm twisted.
They've no money for shoes
so they walk on blisters.
A person whose heart is big,
with an insatiable lust for figs.

Stripped of their former glory,
how many of us tell the same old story?

They'd wake up in the night screaming,
because of the horrible things
that they'd been dreaming.

They'd twitch badly at the smallest sound,
used to the noise of bombs destroying the ground.
Someone not past the point of saving,
but for a period of peace they are craving.

The land of my father - would be
a person so irrevocably changed,
if you didn't know them, you might
think them deranged.
A person who lost a leg or an arm
and has viewed the world through prison bars.

A person capable of great things -
they've got a lovely voice when they sing…
A person whom I wish I knew better
and had kept in touch more by email,
phone call, text message or letter.

Someone whom I wish I could help,
someone whose picture is on my shelf.
A person who was abandoned by their friends,
other people who know how to pretend.

Someone who was bullied at school,
a person who has been labeled a fool.
A person with a tendency to self-harm
and is all too used to raising the alarm.

One of those people who you feel sorry for,
but when they come knocking
you don't open the door.
Someone who has struggled for much of their life
and has a neighbour who just wants to fight.

Someone who has been driven out of their home,
someone who feels that they are alone.
A person who nowadays looks disheveled
and at whom false charges have been levelled.

A person who has done
terrible things through desperation,
someone who rarely feels elation.
One who speaks a beautiful language
and would never turn down
a falafel and humus pita sandwich.

Someone who I love very much,
despite their baggage that fact remains as such.
Unfortunately, Palestine is not a person but a place,
that I hope one day, can wear a smile on its face.

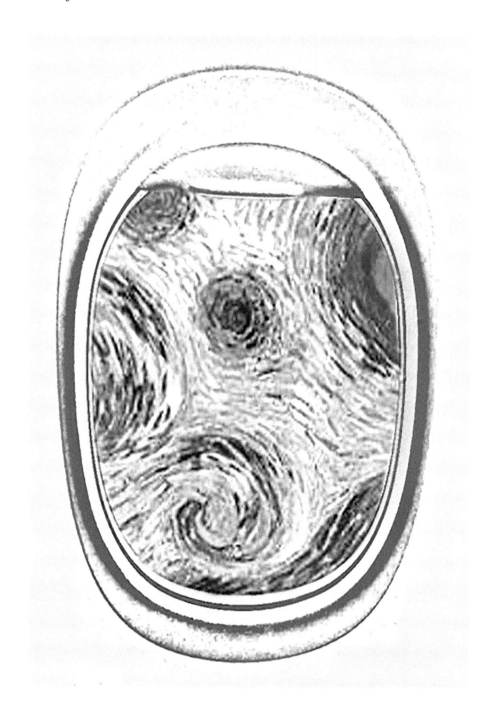

BLURRED STARS

The lens on my camera is broken.
There's no one on board
to hear my thoughtless joking.
No puff on board for when
I'm dying to be smoking.
I tried to push the rock
but the hill was sloping.

Trying to feel happy but 'cos of
my lack of view I'm moping.
There was no other transport available
for when I felt like eloping.
Kept trying to breathe
but the pollution was choking.
Now I want to feel the ground again
but I know I'm floating.

Wandering, drifting,
sifting through rubble,
the dark matter
of outer space.
Before I got here I thought
the universe was a peaceful place.
But now I can't see
if that blue sphere is Earth
or the planet of the apes.

Before I got here
I thought it would be clearer
and we'd left no trace.
But I'm surrounded
by man-made garbage.
It looks tranquil from down below
but really it's carnage.

I only came up here to get a better view,
'cos my telescope was broken,
I couldn't see through.

I was only looking for a postcard picture,
taken on my internal digital camera.
A memorable fixture.

Something to cling onto at night.
A mind's eye view of a beautiful sight.
A crystal clear shot of the dead of night.
But I can't see a thing
the stars are too bright.

All rugged and blurry.
I only wanted to see
the Milky Way from within
before I hit thirty.
But my lens is not working.
It's almost like the light of a fire twerking.
As if from my telescope
the view is intentionally swerving.

But I know one thing for certain.
That dark murky curtain
still fills me with magic.
Although this technologically
handicapped equipment
makes my view so horrifically tragic.
The night sky so atomically tangled,
my perspective irrevocably mangled.

Finally, I emerge from the dream.
I rush to the windows of my shuttle
but they're clouded with steam.

Reality can't surely be
what that sleep induced trauma seemed?
I better just check the sky for closure,
one last look at space before I get a minute older.

But through the dream world
it appears reality spoke.
And all I'm left with
is blurred stars,
a milky scar
viewed solemnly,
through a warped telescope.

My spaceship is broken,
no way to get home.
No hope.
Floating through space,
the most beautiful sight destroyed.
Just a bunch of blurry lights.

No hope.

Just me
and my thoughts,
blurred stars,
through a
broken telescope.

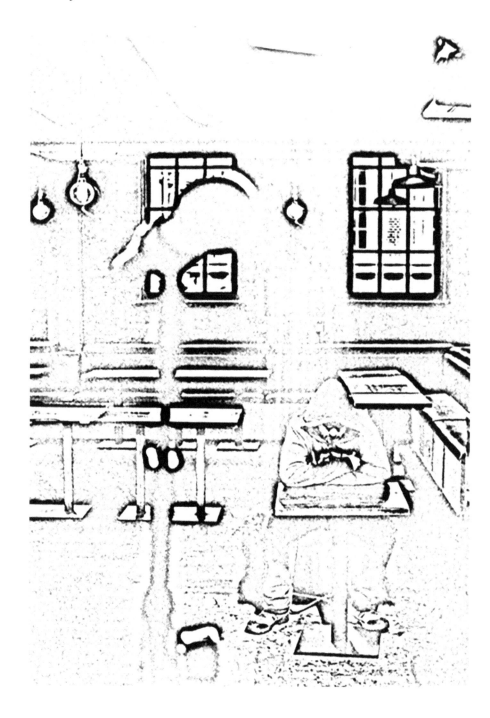

OPEN MIC

There's a buzz, an anticipation.
Like waiting for an away day
train at the station.
Wondering if the next poem
will make me laugh or cry
or feel good vibrations.
Sometimes they make me feel elation,
other times consternation.
I like to reflect on my own situation
by listening to someone else's
perspective or inclinations.

Getting nervous now,
I'm gonna be up soon.
Damn, when will
they call my name?
I guess I'm to blame
for these feelings
I'm about to share.
The shame, the joy,
the anguish, the pain.

It all comes out.
Sometimes I speak softly,
sometimes I shout.
Another bout of my emotions.
We're all here for the devotion
to the words, to our bars
in this downtown bar.
Some came out in the train,
some in the car.
We're dedicated.

The feature made me laugh.
The other artistry was constituted
of dedicated craft
and full of character.
It sets us up nicely.
When I get on stage
I roll the dice as to whether
the audience will like me.

Another pint, another shot,
some Dutch courage.
Yes, yes!
Whose ready for this lyrical flurry?
Oh wait, that's my name...

Here we go,
I try to stand tall, I pray to God
I don't fall.
"How's it going everyone?
My name's Sammy
and this poem's called..."

THE RHYTHM OF LONDON

The provincial came on the train
to find his fortune.
He came listening
on his headphones
to his own beat,
with his own rhythm
locked into his dancing feet.

He stands on the pavement,
a wasp in a beehive.
He looks down
at his loose fitting jeans,
simple skate shoes,
his relaxed manner.
No uptight walk to fit into place,
he feels like a tourist from outer space.

He wonders if the people here really
spend so much of their time underground.
And why the pilots of this hub
who carry the financial world,
but work underground all day
like blood diamond slaves,
are demonized by the media
for wanting a better wage.
"Give them every penny they ask for"
a northerner says.

It's the rhythm of London, the beat of London
we all dance to it, we have no choice.
We often drive to it, or cycle to it.
It's not the kind of place
that wants to hear your voice.
A swirling vortex of people, thoughts, emotions.

A super beehive ever expanding,
the queen bee ever demanding.

Hear the rhythm of London, the beat of London,
you all dance to it, you have no choice.
If you can make it here you can make it anywhere,
I guess it's just making it that's the problem.
Here we need to insert a definition of made.
I would say it's fulfilling your potential,
whatever that is, whoever you are.
No matter what the mediocre driven society
or celebrity obsessed newspapers say.

Feel the rhythm of London, the beat of London,
they all dance to it, they have no choice.
A summered five ringed frenzy engulfed us.
The intensity, the adulation,
the lust for gold
and social admiration.
Fear, hope, disappointment,
anger, envy and heartbreak
for those who don't come top.
The king a yellow flame
who goes too fast to stop.

Dance to the rhythm of London, the beat of London,
we all have to, we have no choice.
The blue madness engulfed us in May,
it couldn't have come too soon
the blue hearts would say.
I guess most never thought
they'd see the day.
On an oligarch's money
that kingdom was made,
or bought I should say.
A modern society with its modern bling,
but still old empirical ways.

Those who lap up success won't complain,
those locked in jealousy want to
go back to the old days.

It's the rhythm of London, it's the beat of London.
we all dance to it, we have no choice.
People talk a lot of economic depression,
I rather think it's a social recession.
Material lust resulting in iphone obsession,
too many causes of which to give
each one a mention.
The collective conscious awaits in
a juvenile detention.
Constantly looking at the phone or the floor,
looking up only enough to get
through the tube door.
A grave disconnection from the community,
this personified London could improve itself
so much if only it had unity.

The rhythm of London, the beat of London,
as far as the eye can see, choice less dancers.
Some self-perceived repressed people
sit in an affluent café.
Do you know what they talk about?
Do you know what they say?
They wonder when they'll see the day
they get all of 'their' land back,
which they've never been to
and is thousands of miles away.
Not far from that place
the diaspora stays.
You know what they talk about
you know what they say.
They wonder when they'll get their land back
and why they had to move,
thousands of miles away.

To the rhythm,
to the beat.
The provincial walks
down the street,
it's a foggy London night.
Not uptight, but upright.
Has he made it?
Hard to say.
But that rhythm
of London still plays,
it's very own Harlem shake.
It plays to keep us dancing,
tasking,
romancing.
For you see it has to,
it has no choice.

A BUS SO BLUE

I wait at a lonely bus stop,
filled with both hope and trepidation.
In my satchel just a lunchbox
and new teacher aspirations.

The bus pulls up, a 219?
Can't be, this one's not red but rather blue.
The smiling driver's from south London,
I drive to parts Chelsea through and through.

The people nod and smile,
they kindly welcome me aboard.
The conductor is a friendly chap
who conveniently lives next door.

Now this bus has a rigid schedule,
for it never turns up late.
When it picks me up it's very early
for a man to start the day.

It drives around London,
to dance, sport and poetry competitions.
The advertising on the side
sells children's dreams and visions.

The passengers are not just any old,
they are a talented group.
They are the feisty, determined types
who like to see things through.

We ride between the commons,
never far from Belleville Way.
I'm sure it drives all night,
but from its path it never strays.

The bus drives across to Finland,
Shanghai and Arizona.
I confess I've always had a secret dream
to drive us all to sunny Barcelona.

My ride was both smooth and bumpy.
The route flew by so fast.
At times I'd cling on so nervously,
like a storm-drenched sailor to the mast.

Yet I leave a seat so worn but comfy,
for the next I've kept it warm.
There's another waiting for me somewhere,
although of its colour I am unsure.

As I pack my things and clear my desk
to head for pastures new,
it occurs to me I would not
have asked for anyone else
to have been sat next to, instead of you.

So I shed a tear and force a smile
before dancing off to my merry beat.
And I can't help but think about
that lonely stop out there,
where someone waits to take my seat.

For the wheels will keep on turning,
as if I was never here.
The fuel hope and ambition
for the next academic year.

I see my stop one final time,
I ring the bell with a smile and cheery wave.
Lonely footsteps echo through the junction,
to the bus so blue, I bid good day.

SPARK

A tiny spark is born and lit,
then drifts off into the ether.
Both fear and wonder fuel the fire
and helps it breathe easier.

Where it lands and rests its head
no-one can truly know.
But the fire lights a distant night
as it burns onwards so slow.

The spark flies through the stormy night,
all it needs is to find a seed.
With nurture, water, food and light,
it has potential to grow a tree.

Who we are and who we hope to be
will be shown clear enough in time.
As sure as the lonely satellite
connects our unruly rhymes.

The hope, the fuel that burns so bright
puts the past into perspective.
Both the lessons learned and disregarded,
depends on the mood selected.

Could I be the one, the shining knight
to bring together feelings torn asunder?
Is this the hope that's meant to be,
or another fateful blunder?

The sky answers no questions.
The stars say neither yes nor no.
But the shooting one's a gesture,
to the beautiful, blurry glow.

The tree that stands ten feet tall
was born through one such spark.
It heard the cry, the will, the call
across the sea so dark.

Through the night the seed is floating
Never stopping until it's ready.
To keep one's nerve, one's hope, one's drive,
requires a ship so steady.

The spark is blowing in the breeze,
one way or another.
For the forest houses many trees,
under that starry, blurry cover.

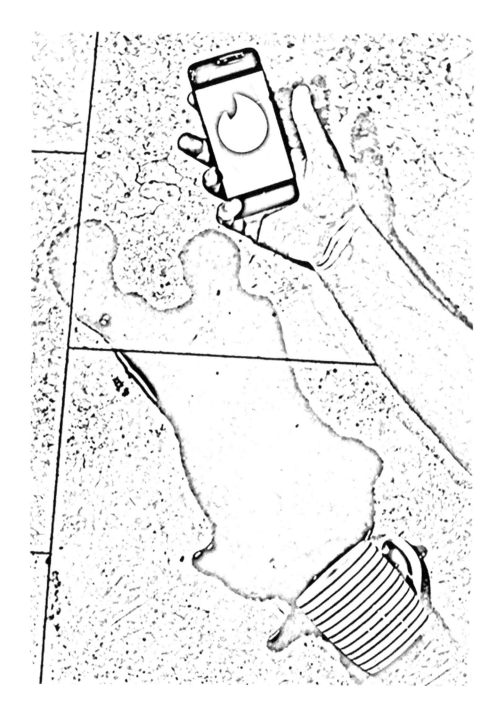

A SUNDAY CUP OF TEA

I'll never forget
that cup of tea
you made me.

It was a Sunday.
It was sweet,
it was strong,
the kind of brew
for which I long.
It was an ordinary Sunday.
I was just a regular guy
who had it all.
But Lord knows the mighty
don't always know
when they're about to fall.

That cup of tea highlights
how well you knew me.
I thought we were soul-mates
like the roots and the trees.
I thought we were interconnected
like honey and bees.
I thought we longed for each other
like the birds and the southern seas.

I knew you were going away for a break,
and I know that sometimes we reach the threshold
of the shit that we can take.
It was when you told me you weren't coming back
that it hit me, like a bird flying
across the train tracks.

You said that there's no solution
so I guess that's the cause of this revolution.

I knew you had things you want to achieve,
in our dreams in life of course we have to believe.
I just thought that we had
some dreamy common ground,
'cos on a day-to-day level
we got on so sound.

But the look in your eyes told me that this time
there'll be no chance of reconciliation.
My soul felt like it was in a state of liquidation,
my heartstrings felt pulled
to the point of inflammation.
I couldn't comprehend the situation,
I felt frustration.

But it's all good!
'Cos now they tell me
it's all about internet dating,
where impressions are based
on a one to five star rating.
I'll tell you what I think of
interweb based matchmaking,
I find it pretty damn humiliating.
I'm like 'Oh great another web forum
to talk shit about myself'.
My profile reads like this:
'My name's Sammy; I'm only here
'cos I just got put back on the shelf'.

I wish I could do that web date stuff
and build it up slowly,
exchange a million emails before you feel like
you've 'got to know me'.
Everyone who knows me will tell you
that's not the case.
I like to talk to people face to face,
I need to intermingle on a personal level

with the human race.
When I left the game I swear
it wasn't so complicated,
when did the female form get so pixelated?
I hate phone calls, text messages and false emails,
a good letter has to be thought about
to tell a good tale.
But nowadays that seems to be an unacceptable
means of communication
in these days of instant bollocks, sorry thoughts,
posted via social networks
resulting in constant handheld device vibration.

Whoever invented this is a massive berk.
The crap my 'friends' put on Facebook
makes me wanna go berserk,
always changing their web face.
My internet personality
I want to erase.
I need to distance myself from
the sound of the phone ring,
not enough sounds do I hear birds singing.
Most days I wanna put
my laptop straight in the bin,
but you know I can't - it's a Macbook Pro
and it's fucking bling.

I'm into whirlwind romances,
I like midnight moon-dances.
I wanna see the moonlight reflect
on your beautiful face
out in a field somewhere
to the sound of nature,
or under a strobe and laser
in a rave consisting of, I don't know,
techno or drum and bass.

Anywhere I can whisper sweet poetry in your ear,
not this pre-prepared shit but a freestyle
direct from the heart for you to hear.
You were the only person who appreciated
my spontaneous, spannered rhymes
that only come out so perfectly
at a certain time.
Hell, the only reason I'm on
this reflective vibe
is I'm still blatantly thinking
about you all of the time.
It's getting cloudy up in my mind,
salvation I cannot find.
On top of a vertiginous vortex I live my life.
Constantly on the edge of a cliff,
when I close my eyes
I can still get a whiff of your beautiful scent
my whole life am I doomed to repent?
My ideology seems so suspect.

I thought I only had one regret
in this life that I wish I could say is not true.
But then like you I thought it through,
and like you I've come to conclude
that it's probably best that we're through.

But baby I'll never forget
that cup of tea you made me.
Sweetheart believe me that day
will be forever ingrained into my memory.

You know the one I mean,
that cold November Sunday.
When you got up
and made me that top cup of tea,

then left me.

AVALON (THE LAST LETTER)

I was tired.
Mentally and physically,
spiritually and sensually.

Tired of a lot of things,
tired of not having wings.
Of not being able to just fly away
from the troubles that life brings.

I was tired of being
a puppet on strings,
of being a slave to
modern technological bling.
Tired of being disconnected from nature,
worn down by being
conditioned to be a hater.

I was bedraggled
by the constant
sound of the grinding.
Tired of constantly looking, reflecting,
soul-searching but not finding.

I was forlorn by the attitudes
of those around me.
I was exhausted by
the continuous struggles
which surrounded me.

I was tired of not
having the answer.
Tired of the questions
that eat away inside
like a cancer.

Tired of being constantly put down.
My facial muscles were drained
by having to constantly
wear a frown.

I was shattered by
the emptiness inside.
So much lost and gone
from which I used to thrive.

I was tired of thinking of you.
All that relentless energy wasted
on wondering why
we couldn't see it through.

Left weary by the storm
that we weathered.
Empty and cold inside
by thoughts of
times we spent together.

Exhausted by thoughts
of the future.
When I get there
I hoped to rest
in an Avalon so super.

You said I have a lot
to learn about love,
I guess we both do.
In the end we couldn't fly
like two white doves
we couldn't see it through.

I just hoped time will heal
the pain of losing you.
Although from your reactions
and demeanor I'm guessing onwards
you've already moved.

A little selective perspective
was what I was needing,
an escape from the heartache
that I was feeling.

Like the movement of the ocean
the anguish slowly receded,
from the tidal wave of emotions
and internal bleeding.

I would sit thinking
of us together
in our little palace,
before our love became
a poisoned chalice.

Through all of the troubles
and problems I thought
we could manage.
How could we allow our love
to sustain such
irreparable damage?
To the point where now
memories of you,
I just want to banish.

So I'm just here with
my bars, my words.
At least a part of me
they make a third,

I don't need you
but I need some girl.
I don't know who
you are anymore,
don't be getting
your boys in the rave
to be throwing looks
at me like that.
What was that for?
You want the attention,
you need to be in detention.
The way your mind works
is reminiscent of dementia,
all thinking backward.
But I guess you were right when
you left because you
thought it wouldn't work.
Well guess what?
It wouldn't work, didn't work, wasn't working.
I hope you feel vindicated because
your memory is now getting pixilated.

When I saw you the other day for the
first time in nine months I didn't feel frustrated.
I still don't understand why you were
looking over here,
chatting shit about me like you'd
still contemplate it.

You can go be
whoever you want to be,
I can only ever be me.
A new version of
that same person
who was sitting there
that cold wintry day
when you left me.

So here I am one year on,
check it out
I'm going strong.
That fatigue for you
is long gone.
That feeling symptomatic
of a notion so wrong.

With you I know
I surely didn't belong.
But when you left that day
you set me free,
you left me strong.
Positive balance and recreation
have been the source of my salvation.
Now I'm free to experience
true elation.
The devastation felt
when you went that day
has moved aside
has slipped away.
You're gone from the bloodstream,
no traces left.
You left me bereft
but stronger than ever.
Trust me chic
I've recouped,
I've got my thing together.
Any day, any weather
the sun still shines in my heart,
you can't kill that with your
verbal Berettas.
I got sold down the river
by cupid and his poisoned quiver.
But emotionally I'm not cold,
I don't shiver.

It's been one hell of a year.
But as I remember you
I shed no tears.
For the future,
I have no fears.

So here I am
one year on.
Still searching for my Avalon.
But trust me darling,
you're long gone.

Sammy Nour

▲

SILENCE

Awkward silence
more powerful
than violence.
Especially when you
use it as a
weapon.

This is important,
say something,
anything.

Break the monopoly
of my words,
my thoughts.
The stream of
consciousness is endless.

And still nothing.

The silence is like
a black hole in
deep space.

Sucking all in.

I can't play
the game when
you do this.
I have no weapon.
Disarmed.
All the wisdom I had

before this 'conversation' dismantled.
Effortless destruction on your part,
that was easier than
breaking a piece of Ikea furniture
that was put up on a come down.

I beseech thee,
come down.
Come down from
that high horse.
You see now all
of my remorse.

Come down.
Or don't.

Just fucking
say something.

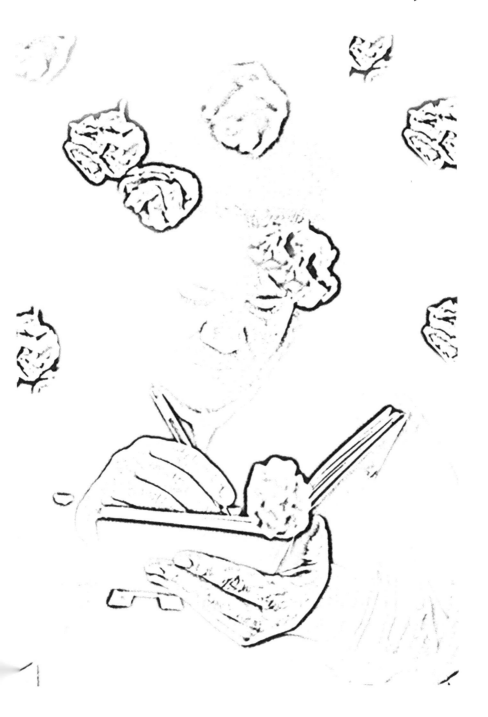

THE LONELY POET

My tongue is tied
my lips are dry.
I have no ticket
to board this ride.

My pen is dead
my book is read.
The thought of joining words
fills me with dread.

I have no soul
I am not whole.
A hanger swinging
after the garment's been stole.

An empty glass
an unattended class.
Just plain Gordon
without the flash.

A wheel-less car
a dying star.
An empty cave
a silent rave.
A soldier,
who is not brave.

An evening lunch
a nighttime brunch.
I am the captain
without the crunch.
The monster stoned
without his munch.

An empty bird's nest
a model naked with no clothes to dress.
A paper without any copy to press.
A board without any pieces for chess.
A crash test dummy that's never seen duress.

I am dog without an owner,
words were my friends.
Now I'm a loner.
A lime without a Corona,
an empty grinder with no stoner.
It's like watching porn without a boner.

I'm a pea without a pod
a lodger without a lodge.
A pint without the top
a warehouse without a shop.
The home stand without the kop.
A breakdown without the drop.
An endless brick wall -
when will it stop?

Romeo with no Juliet.
A credit card without debt.
I am the mush without the peas.
An evergreen that has no leaves.
I live in the forest that has no trees.

I am the razzle without the dazzle.
Shampoo with no conditioner,
that's why my hair's all frazzled.

I am the train without the track
I am subtlety with no tact.
The nineteenth hole without the course.
The morning, without a dawn.

I am the bed without the room.
I am the trip but with no 'shrooms.
I am the clown without the face.
I am the rat without the race.
The show without the practice.
The non-praying Godless mantis.

I feel like the mouse when the cat
had to go to the vet 'cos he had diarrhea
and kept shitting all over the house.

I just want to write a fucking poem!
Oh wait…

ODE TO PEDLEY

Today we mourn
the original Punk Panther bassist.
Known around Leicester in the more unusual places.
A real life character, a man of many faces.
Loved by many, remembered by all.
With him you never quite knew what was in store.
Heartbreak in the end, was he too afraid?
'What could anyone have done?' is the question today.
It's always saddening to hear of the death of another.
A son, a loved one, a friend, a brother.
This one's for you, pal, I raise the glass high.
To those whose sun shines that much dimmer
since the day you died.
As you were also a ball of blazing flame.
A real human of joy, of sorrow, of pain.
You weren't my best mate, but PPST crew.
Only the good times will I choose to remember of you.
But all that's irrelevant now,
I hope the suffering's gone in your journey anew.

REALITY TV

If you turn on the TV during the day,
Everyone around knows
what's coming your way.
Morning, midday and afternoon.
If you're watching them all
you're probably not heading
out to work soon.

If you like to laugh at
the weak and the damned,
you're probably tuning in
to see who tries their hand.
Burberry caps, stripy tops
and 90's trackies,
a shower of chavy fanatics
who often act manic.

Whilst most of us are out,
hard at work,
you can watch grown adults
behaving like burks.

Do you like to be voyeuristic
and see people with no coping skills?
Are you sat at home all day
while the state pays your bills?
As you peer on the dregs
of a dysfunctional society,
you're sat at home on the sofa,
are you in a state of sobriety?

In that case you're watching TV – reality style!
No matter how much you hate it,
you can't help but smile.

For a human creation it's exceptionally vile,
as it puts victims and perpetrators on televised trial.
It loves itself and thinks its ratings are justified,
for the grilling it gives people
who chew gum with their mouths open wide.

Barneys, DNA and lie detector tests,
The host's arrogance, you know the rest.
Constantly reminding us
that's his name up in lights,
but really he's a prime-time Don King,
promoter of fights.

Roll up to see how your taxes get spent.
See how people who've
made mistakes promise to repent.
That is of course unless the
lie detector tests come back negative,
if you watch it all the time
it becomes quite repetitive.

OK, sometimes he goes for the soppy stories.
But let's face it the viewers find them boring.
They tune in to see it all kick off,
I'm surprised they don't issue
the contestants with Kalashnikovs.

Everyday the strapline
and stories are the same.
Unfortunately on society
some of these people are a drain.
Who's to blame?
As you watch it, do you feel ashamed?

"Do you need our help?
Like to be on the show?
Give us a call, come and have a go!"
Translated:
"Come on the show
so I can call you scum.
I like nothing better than to
watch you kick off with your mum."

You can have his help
backstage and beyond
So long as you'll join
this televised throng.
So long as you'll agree to
go on TV and be publicly humiliated,
Our sponsors love that
it's mainstream facilitated.

The advert breaks tell me
to call injury lawyers for compensation.
As my car insurance just went up,
for me this is a major source of frustration.
Is this really the state of
our modern sophisticated society?
You know you can't help but watch
with a sense of self satisfaction and piety.

I hear you ask why I'm watching
this nonsense anyway?
Well it's just the life of
a lonely teacher, on school holidays.

IMMIGRATION

Registering at immigration,
you'd think it would be an easy job.
Now I know I'm British
and we love bureaucracy.
And as a foreigner in this fine land,
I don't want you to think I'm a knob.

But fucking hell.
I get told to come down here
to get a number on a piece of paper.
I tell you,
it would be easier
to get sky diving lessons
from Nelson Mandela
and I hate you.

I sit outside in the street all morning,
cursing the sight of your office
as the day is dawning.
Then senior jobsworth copper
'too shit for the beat' comes out
about 9 o'clock to distribute some tickets.
I've been here so long
I'm malnourished.
I've probably got rickets.
(But I'll take a glass of orange juice
if you've got one).

But no, now I've got to chill
in your waiting room.
Bathing happily in the smell of sandals
infused with doom.
Watching the numbers crawl by,

'only fifty more to go!'
a forlorn cellmate cries.
But I'm ever the optimist,
I crack a joke.
You know me,
always trying to make the most.
But my smile dies a death
as the door creaks open
and a rather scary
looking woman emerges.
'Do you want anything
from the pharmacy?',
she casually asks co-workers.
'No we good but you go ahead,
it's not as if this room is full
of impatient foreign bellends'.
I'm thinking by the time
I get out of here,
I'll probably be dead.

'Whatcha mean the
fucking pharmacy?,
you finish at 2 o'clock!
You have all day to
do your errands
and sort your life out
you lazy sod'.
Although sure bet
when you get home
you'll have a moan
to whoever
about the strife.

Hours go by I wonder
why you can't just give me
that piece of paper.

Why do you continue
to keep me here
in this sadistic game.
Trapped forever in this
world of bureaucracy
gone insane.
More hours go by, she comes back
laughing to herself proudly
at the room full of waiting twats.

More hours lost,
my number comes
I'm finally to be seen.
As the door opens
to the inner sanctum
I walk towards the light,
is this a dream?

They say 'vale, muy bueno.
Now go to the bank,
pay your tenner
then come back tomorrow'.
I said 'Whatcha mean?'
Then she looked in
my poor naïve British eyes
and said 'What did you think
this would be done by October?
You joker!
This groundhog day's
gonna be repeating itself
over and over and over.
Don't sweat it, come back tomorrow
and get your stamp.
I'll give you temporary relief.
But you'll be back soon again, sunshine,
so you better bring some strong ass weed'.

Fuck that. Team chat.
In the huddle, we decide: bank run.
Let's chance it, we come back.
And I can tell you now
the boss's patience
is getting slack
when there's no
more tickets left.
Oh man this can't be,
I can hear the lady's voice
laughing in my head,
as the thought of
coming back tomorrow
is making me bereft.
'Haha come back tomorrow
so I can devastate you'
I think as I kick the wall
in frustration,
still seeking that elusive piece of paper.

We need to get some Tories in here,
they'll be sure to sort out this mess.
A job for life, we'll see about that
as we watch your annual review progress.
But that's just a distant dream right now,
one of many symptoms of my frustration.
As I sit seriously contemplating homicide
out the back of Estacion del Norte train station.

But when I have my way I swear to God
I'll burn this office to the ground,
as the cheer of dishevelled foreigners
remains the only sound.
I send seven plagues on it
or smash it with a bulldozer.

That is of course if I get out of here
before hell has frozen over.
Roll up in a JCB, in fact not one but three.
'Cos I know Stace and Kerrie and all the gang
will want to be there with me.

Until then I dream of angry lynch mobs,
armed with wires, monitors and routers.
Who'll replace all you useless shits
with a room full of computers.

ARE COUNTRY

In this Brexit,
we blame the foreigners.
This incessant bullshit,
we let it bother us
"Dodge the taxes"
Proclaim the elite.
Old plastic face
in charge of the trees.
A cheese topped monkey
defames Iran.
Gold turns to copper
at the touch of his hand.
Black Friday consumes the masses.
Nine thousand pounds
university classes.
British ministers
controlled by Israel.
Nazis are now activists.
Our musical heroes
slit their wrists.
There are numbers
hidden in paradise.
Sexual assault
is normal not rife.
Inequality of gender pay.
Artificial intelligence
in the leader's face.
The voters nearly
made a change.
Of clothing that is,
the emperor's name.
Terrorist attacks
in the run up to elections.

Coincidentally just as Labour
were gaining momentum.
Interest on
the mortgage squeezed.
The earth it costs
for a household feed.
Foodbanks scorch the land.
In ruins lies
a generation's plan.
A mountain of debt
is there to climb.
Or a cobbled doorway
infused with wine.
Just be grateful for
(insert quote here)
say the remoaners
and brexiteers.

A health service
in the depths of despair.
A socialist ideal
in capitalism's glare.
A wage squeeze,
civil servants
act like Oliver begging
"Can I have enough
to live on please?"
Fake news
flies through the air.
A wigged muppet
is the USA's compere.
Grown up children
argue publicly
and threaten
nuclear war unjustly.
Just dickheads

with small cocks
and shit haircuts.
Nothing to see here,
just a pre-scripted pantomime
designed to induce fear.
Russia meddles.
The Daily Press peddles
hate and slander
alongside nationalist rebels.
Global warming heats the Earth.
Satirical memes
give us mirth.
A Christmas ad
with Muslim family,
causes much
internet profanity.
Connect online
and be offended.
Be a hypocrite,
ever pretending.
As even Bono betrayed
our trust.
Tax dodgers
on Children in Need
say giving's a must.
Believe the news
you'll know
that Palestinians
occupy stolen land,
not Jews.
Always make sure
you recycle.
But buy the biggest car
you can,
not a bicycle.
Apply values

When it suits you,
only care about
your children's future.

Britain used to be a place
more equal, whether you were
white, Asian or black.
But hey,
this is Brexit.
We have our country back.

TWENTY SIX POUNDS SEVENTY P

Twenty six pounds seventy p.
I only wanted to go to Leicester
from Liverpool lime street.
Crammed in the bike compartment
of the train like a sardine.
Is this what it means to be fast and free?
They promised privatized public services
would boost the economy.
You know what I see?
I see the government selling out
you and me to the corporate machine.
I see politicians taking corporate hospitality
in return for government policy
that benefits multinational companies.
So now we got British railways
owned by fuckers in Germany.
We got Spain creating monopolies
dominating public services economies
in Latin America.
I thought the west was supposed
to give up colonial ties.
I thought to empires of old we waved bye-bye.
Hell they made the UK give up ours
after the second world war.
What was that for?
So now the EU can fuck them over
with their Leading world economy turnover.
Little farmers overseas
ain't got a chance against the big three.
Thanks to the common agricultural policy
which gives out fancy farming subsidies.
So the French can make a million types of cheese
and the elite get in on the freebies

by getting cash for owning half our country.
Ah this glorious European community,
not a hint of capitalist critique.
It oversees this corporate spree
and contrives to fuck over you and me.

We need to move away from America and
their ideology, religion and market perspectives.
Rational they seem to have neglected.
We need to stop them,
their actions have affected
all of us for too long.
Our economy's strong but we don't belong
in their suicidal trade regime.
We can't trade dollars for more trees.
They refuse to consider
developing sustainable technology.
They just wanna drill for oil in arctic seas
and fuck over third world economies.
Start pointless wars far overseas
and intervene where it ain't our beeswax.
Hell they blagged our main man
to use our tax to kill
innocent people in Iraq and
cause a bloody civil war
then try and bring 'our boys' back.
But our boy's finished now
he's nice and relaxed.
Living off his corporate payoffs
and buying mansions down south.
We gave him the mandate,
we put him in charge.
Our faith in our beloved
democracy was large.
Next thing you know he's been
bought off by the USA.

Lets save the day!
Lets even blag that they got WMDMAs
If they did we should know
we sold them the bastards.
Our man talks shit about Lazarus.
Middle east envoy my arse.
You go where your sent
by your corporate masters.
To make things look good,
they pay you in cash.

But what can I do?
I'm just a consumer.
To go against hegemony
I must be a looner.
So I just watch Matt Damon
and pretend he can act.
I buy the daily paper to see if
his love-life's still intact.
We don't protest anymore
like we did with the poll tax.
When the government tried to axe off
some more of our cash.
That's what we need,
riots in the streets.
It's the only way to be heard
by the government machine.
And the sneering bureaucracy
lurking behind the scenes.
Thinking how they can divert public money
away from its needs.
How they can maintain the status quo.
They don't wanna know
where we think they're going wrong.
If we burn down their plush offices
they'll start hearing our song.

Don't wanna be owned by corporations,
wanna live with thought and motivation.
Rather than being numbed
by their control manifestations.
Wanna live with earth appreciation
and help needy brothers without reservation.
Only by leading through demonstration
that we can balance world economic relations
does our world have a chance of finding salvation
and bringing prosperity to all of its nations.

For years we've had patience
with supranational creations
which have just overseen
the united devastation of nations
and just deal with the situation
by making false proclamations
to impoverished nations
they put in the situation.
There's no arbitration
or trade regulation,
just chronic manipulations
of imperial infestations.
Who say it's Islam and communism
that are causing sensations.

Twenty six pounds seventy p.
Fuckin hell,
I only wanted to go from Leicester
to Liverpool lime street.
Ended up ranting about the corporate machine.

RISE OF THE MACHINES

Anyone remember 8 track?
I sure as hell don't
(Come on I'm not that old).
Let's face it, it was whack.
But... the older brother
of our beloved cassette!

Anyone remember cassette?
To that small piece of plastic we are all in debt.
It gave us the freedom to record our own tunes
and make our own mixtapes.
We were over the moon!
Remember crouched by your tape player?
Waiting for the DJ on the radio
to drop your favourite tune.
If you pressed record at the
wrong second you might regret it.
As you'd catch the selector telling you
what he reckons.

Remember those tapes?
You only had forty-five minutes
of tunes you could play.
And you had to take the thing out
and switch it around!
It was the only way.
Remember fast forwarding to
hear your favourite sounds?
And when the damn things broke
you'd have to spend ten minutes
with a pencil, or worse your finger
putting the tape back together.
Just what you needed when
walking home in cold weather.

Remember when we clipped
walkmans to our belts?
When you fell off your
skateboard your music died
You nearly cried out
and you cursed like hell.

Anyone remember minidisc?
Dropping that was like a game of risk.
For about ten minutes
they were all the rage.
With their little mini inside cage
they were that small, losing it was a ball.
We'd never seen anything close
to these pieces of plastic,
man they were fantastic.
Musically they were hench
with their super mini strength.

I guess what I'm talking about
is the rise of the machines.
I won't even get into CDs
'cos nowadays, shiny ipods
and ipads are the things of our dreams.
But be careful, those mini computers
are more than they seem.
Now I can check my emails
whilst listening to music.
And now all of big tech know
everything about me.

As far as 'piracy' goes,
I don't have a wooden leg and a parrot
in case you're not in the know.
We don't call it stealing we call it sharing,

'cos for all those years
the music industry was uncaring.
Twenty five pounds for a cd!
Screw you, high street and
your 'American imports'.
They had us by the balls.
Now I just go online
to find sublime.
At the click of a button
no music can hide.

But the abuse didn't stretch to only the consumer,
it was the artists and performers
who were really the losers.
On the sales of all those expensive CDs
the artists only made a small percentage piece.
Now the record labels got
the cheek to call us the thieves!
If you're a drummer in a band
you're probably on a salary, not royalties.
And you're mistaken if you think
streaming sites pay the artists properly.
Most musicians just want their stuff
out there, they don't care.
They're seeking retribution
we don't need distribution.
Nowadays all you need is
an internet connection,
to the theft of the past
there's coming correction.
Real fans will still come see your shows,
buy your t-shirts
and show you the love
'cos they're in the know.
Fuck you record execs.
I hope you're out on your arse

with nowhere to go.
You ripped us off for so long.
But with or without the internet
the music scene will always be strong.

So here's the message
to all big money artists
who complain about piracy.
You're hypocrites,
'cos you're putting your videos
for free on your socials hoping
for your tune to go viral, see?
You should be grateful
you're making a living playing music.
You got love from the fans,
don't be greedy.
Don't abuse it.

And what's the difference between
streaming legit and illegal ways?
Legit is cool and is a free
marketing mouthpiece
for what the record labels say.
I could go on all day.

Anyone remember vinyl?

THE POLITICIAN AND THE TEACHER

Shut up you little teacher,
what do you know?
I'm in the marginally-elected government
and what I say goes.
You've seen my changes
and beneficial reforms.
You seen me in the news
so surely you know.
I don't care if you've
been doing it for years.
You're a fucking tit.
In a paranoid, limbo and idiotic state,
you're refusing to change.
You don't think what I'm doing is right
you must be insane.
I like to demonise you in the media.
And spread untrue rumours
about you on sickopedia.
I'm part of the establishment
that lost the dossier on pedophilia.
I induce false moral panics
to make the population act so manic.
Anything I can I will use.
If it's your life story
or your deepest blues.
A soldier getting
hacked up in the street
is perfect for me.
As it meets the criteria
for justifying a UK Patriot Act.
And it's a known fact that

I use the human suffering
of my inferiors
for my own ends.
I'll cause you confusing hysteria.
Our party only has
one policy; that's cuts,
if you're NHS, teaching or army
you're out of luck.
I gotta take your wages and pension
and give it to the banks.
But in the long run trust me,
my buddies will thank me.

You're all getting clipped.
My idea to motivate you
is to beat you with a whip.
Until you give into
me slashing your
pay and conditions.
I'm in the political division.
I'll take your profession apart
like a mortician.

At the end of the day,
when the next generation look
back at history.
They'll remember my name,
but your gravestone will be blank.
It will read no one, nothing.
A lowly teacher, a mystery.

Settle down politician,
what do you know?
Why, I didn't elect you
into government, you have
well and truly shown.
And don't talk to me

about power trips,
'cos in the classroom
what I say goes.
I've seen your absurd changes
and detrimental reforms.
I've seen you in the news,
I recognize your Pinoccio nose.

By the way, you go ahead
and take us down through
your friends and op-ed
pieces in the media.
We're all too busy to take notice
trying to turn children
into encyclopedias.
And we can all take a joke,
we've all read sickopedia.
But you're just the same
as the last politician
and the ones before.
Like the liars in the other party
who conspired to drag us to war.
You loved that soldier getting
hacked up in the street
but you prefer worse.
Trust me though,
the justice for the men
your kind send to their deaths
will one day be served.

So you carry on dragging us
through the mud.
One day trust me
justice will be done.
Sinners will be blinded
by the light of the final sun.

Your time will come,
the struggle will be won.

You know what, you're right.
At the end of the day,
when the next generation
looks back at history,
they may not remember our names.
But through the population
our influence will surely be plain.
We'll leave something
you can never give.
My blank grave will be associated with
hope, peace, education and love.
We subscribe to a philosophy
you'll never understand.
'Cos it doesn't conform to
the ideals of your dominant hegemony.

It's called trying to
make the world a better place.
Changing young lives,
shaping young minds.

A positive legacy.

TOP DOG

I just want to say thank you
for all of your loving words.
Such heartfelt speech
is seldom ever heard.
What you said made me feel
so much better about life,
especially when I'm
going through this strife.
You're the only person
in whom I can truly confide,
no disrespect to the girls
that I've had in my life.
You understand me
and between us there are no lies.

No matter how hard we try
this life is never easy.
This rollercoaster ride sometimes
makes me feel queasy,
which is why I am so thankful to you.
Because you're the person
who always helps me through
the tough times, the hard days
and all of the ways God chooses
to test us to see our true ways.

You know that we'll always be there for each other.
Soulmates, friends and blood brothers.
We are so many different things to each other.
I just want to see you be happy,
content in yourself and always laughing.

You're such a truly top person.
I can always depend on you, that is for certain.
I love the way you can cheer me up,
even when my humour circuit is second gear stuck.
We seem to communicate telepathically,
even when we're far away you feel me emphatically.
We're always connected through
some strange force,
that's the way a spiritual connection
can work, of course.

Sometimes we don't speak for days on end.
But through spiritual communication
our thoughts transcend the barriers
of Facebook and mobile phones.
If my phone's dead I cannot feel alone.
Knowing that you're there to guide me,
our deep connection I feel inside of me.

Strange the way things work out.
All of the money you can fork out
could never buy the relationship
we have between us.

'Cos you know that there is no other
you're the only one, top dog.
My friend.
My brother.

CRACKS

It's been a while since
I started hiding things in the wall,
then papering over the cracks.

When cracks would appear in the cracks
I would simply hide more,
then paper over them again.

And when cracks appeared
in the cracks of those cracks,
I knew the walls wouldn't take any more.
So I started hiding things under the floorboards.

It wasn't long before the cellar was full,
so I began putting them under the carpet.
As the basement rose it
eclipsed the light from the window.

Now I can't go in the room anymore.

Already every storage space
in my house was full,
so I started taking things
up to the attic.

One by one.
Box by box.
Piece by piece.
Up that loft ladder.

I arranged them in a haphazard
formation of things
that should have gone,
but were somehow still here.

Things I just couldn't let go of.

Downstairs I barely noticed
the ceiling start to bow.
Little by little.
Inch by inch.
It happened at such a slow pace.
I would walk in a room and it would
would be an inch from my face.
And I would be there still telling myself
it's ok.

I had no idea if it was day or night.
Every window was blocked
so I couldn't open one
to see outside and
scream for help.
When I did all that came back
were whispers from the
things on my shelves.

One night I went in my garden
and started filling my shed.
Not with bikes or tools,
but with things that
should have been dead.
Then the garage, the yard.
No space available for my car.

Back in my house
there was only a tiny space to dwell.
At not one point did I think
to open a window and cry for help.
Or even go outside.

The doors were unlocked
this whole time.

Eventually the cracks became chasms
then the chasms became valleys
and the valleys became tundras.
There was a loud crash
and then rubble
was all I could see.
A hundred thousand pieces of me.

Only then did the sun light up my face.
I turned to true north where
my house had once faced.
And wondered why I ever
started hiding things in the first place.

All I can say is if you live in
a house like mine.
Open the window,
there's still time.

About Sammy

Being of Irish/Palestinian descent, Sammy has always had a keen interest in people, politics and history, and attempts to make sense of these through his poetry. Platform 7 reflects the variety of the experiences he has had and the topics he writes about. A keen traveller, he has set up home in various places around England, Mozambique and Spain. He finds writing cathartic, with poetry a creative way of expressing those feelings we all struggle to articulate in everyday conversation.

Some-Antics, the spoken word event that Sammy co-founded, started over a latte and a pot of raspberry tea. Sammy and his friend Kishan created the open-mic night in a coffee shop in Leicester. They wanted a poetry event with a different kind of vibe to most, including an open mic, slam-poetry, a feature performer and a DJ all in one. An evening that welcomes all through the doors, regardless of age or experience, to create, perform and cook up a storm of words.

Some-Antics is and does just that, and is regarded for its welcoming and inclusive attitude. It strives to be not just an event, but a community of poets, DJs, photographers, videographers and graphic designers, all contributing their time and effort to building and sustaining an artistic community. In addition to the performance event, Some-Antics is host to a Writers' Collective, meeting monthly to write together and connect poets from Leicester and beyond.

Sammy's creativity does not end with writing; he has a passion for music too. Sammy is part of Tongue N Groove, a DJ collective who put on events around Leicester, and has many regular attendees. Sammy has played in various rock and punk bands, contributing to song-writing and playing rhythm and bass guitar.

Sammy is also a teacher. He has taught in primary schools in Leicester, London, Mozambique and Spain. He has helped to set up an inter-school poetry slam competition in south London. Sammy currently teaches students with special needs in his hometown of Leicester. He inspires his students to take in an interest in music and writing, and helps them to believe in their talents by running various music production and performance poetry initiatives.

In his spare time, Sammy loves fantasy games, regularly playing and hosting Dungeons and Dragons sessions. He also enjoys video games and collecting vinyl records. Sammy has a passion for camping and exploring, often spending time driving through the UK and European countrysides in his Volkswagen T4, looking for another adventure to inspire the next poem.

SanRoo Publishing

To find out more about SanRoo Publishing
visit our website at:

www.sanroopublishing.co.uk

Follow us on Facebook @acalltowrite

or on Twitter @SanRooWriters

SanRoo Publishing
is part of
Inspiring You C.I.C

26 Bramble Way, Leicester, LE3 2GY
Registered Company No. : 1021381

Lightning Source UK Ltd.
Milton Keynes UK
UKHW022038020721
386538UK00007B/435